A Family in Greenland

This book takes you on a trip to Kulusuk Island, off the east coast of Greenland. There you will meet the Bajare family, who live in a small village in the ice and snow. Like his ancestors, Harald Bajare is a hunter. He will tell you about the dangers and adventures of the hunter's life. You will also discover how the Bajares spend their time, what they eat, what their interests are, and how life is changing for the people of Greenland.

FAMILIES AROUND THE WORLD

A FAMILY IN
GREENLAND

Peter Otto Jacobsen and
Preben Sejer Kristensen

The Bookwright Press
New York · 1986

Families Around the World

A Family in Australia
A Family in Central America
A Family in Colombia
A Family in China
A Family in France
A Family in Greenland
A Family in Hawaii
A Family in Holland
A Family in Hong Kong
A Family in Iceland

A Family in India
A Family in Ireland
A Family in Japan
A Family in Mexico
A Family in the Persian Gulf
A Family in Switzerland
A Family in Thailand
A Family in the U.S.S.R.
A Family in West Africa

First published in the United States in 1986 by
The Bookwright Press
387 Park Avenue South
New York, NY 10016

First published in 1986 by
Wayland (Publishers) Limited
61 Western Road, Hove
East Sussex BN3 1JD, England
© Copyright 1986 Text and photographs
Peter Otto Jacobsen and Preben Sejer Kristensen
© Copyright 1986 English-language edition
Wayland (Publishers) Limited

ISBN 0–531–18082–4
Library of Congress Catalog Card Number: 85–73584

Phototypeset by Kalligraphics Limited
Redhill, Surrey
Printed in Italy by G. Canale and C.S.p.A., Turin

Contents

Flying across Greenland

We are traveling by plane right across Greenland, from the west coast to the east, to visit the Bajare family. They live on the island of Kulusuk, off the east coast.

Ever since we took off from the airport at Søndre Strømfjord, on the west coast, we have been flying across an endless icy waste. Greenland is the world's largest island, with an area of more than 2,000,000 square kilometers (800,000 square miles). It is also one of the least inhabited areas, and as we look out of the window of the plane it is not difficult to see why.

Most of Greenland lies within the Arctic Circle and is frozen and inhospitable. Snow can fall in any month of the year and, even on the southern tip of the island, temperatures do not rise much above freezing in summer. However, the strip of land around the coast is a little

Much of Greenland is covered in ice and snow all year round.

less frozen, allowing people to settle and a few crops to grow. When the Vikings first sailed here, about 1,000 years ago, they named the island Greenland because of the shrubs and bushes they found growing along the coast.

But there is nothing green in our view from the plane. In fact, we can see very little sign of life. There are only about 130 towns and villages in the whole of Greenland. There are no railroads at all, only a small number of roads, and very few cars. Traveling is usually by plane, helicopter, snowmobile or sled.

We have brought plenty of warm clothing with us. As the plane comes in to land at the small airport at Kulusuk, we prepare ourselves for the bitter weather.

Greenland, the world's largest island, covers an area of 2,175,600 sq. km. (840,000 sq. mi.).

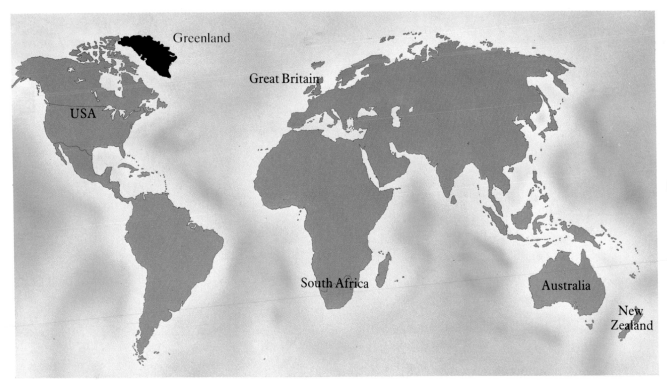

Arriving at Kap Dan

The Bajares live on the island of Kulusuk, which is surrounded by frozen sea throughout the winter.

The Bajare family live at Kap Dan, about 3 kilometers (2 miles) from the airport. We leave the plane and take a ride on a dog sled. The only other way of traveling here is by "snow cats" – special vehicles with caterpillar tracks.

As the dogs pull us across the ice, we see the small settlement of Kap Dan coming into view. There are just 400 people here, living in some 70 wooden cabins. The village also has a wooden church, a store, a school, and a meeting hall. There are no roads, only snow tracks. Outside each house, dogs are chained to the ice. Many of them look more like wolves than dogs, and they certainly howl like wolves.

At once, we set off to meet the Bajares. They are related to the Inuit people (the Eskimos) of North America. Many hundreds of years ago their ancestors traveled to Greenland and settled here. Now, of course, they are Greenlanders and they speak Greenlandic – a dialect of the Inuit language.

Harald Bajare is a hunter. When we arrive at the Bajares' house, Harald is not at home. He's out hunting.

"He's out there," says his wife Batseba, pointing out across the ice, "but he'll be back home soon."

Kulusuk island is off the east coast of Greenland, just below the Arctic Circle.

9

We meet Harald Bajare

We climb a ridge and look out over the ice. The sea around the island is frozen over. Here and there the ice has been

Harald drags the body of a seal behind him as he makes his way home across the ice.

pushed up to form cliffs. Although it is not snowing and there is no wind, the temperature is bitterly cold at about −30°C (−22°F).

Then we notice a black dot in the distance moving slowly toward us. The dot grows larger and we dimly begin to see a smaller dot close behind. It must be Harald, bringing his catch home.

He slowly works his way in toward the coast, across the frozen sea. He is on sealskin-covered skis, dragging a seal after him. As he reaches us, he is greeted by his wife Batseba, who takes charge of the seal. Harald tells us that he has just traveled 20 kilometers (12 miles) across the ice. He caught the seal in a net under the ice. This means there are no bullet holes in it, so they will get a better price for the seal's skin.

Harald and Batseba married five years ago and now have three small sons, Henning, Kristian and Åge. They all live together with Harald's parents, Jonas, who is 58 years old, and Emma, who is 70.

All seven people live off what Harald catches or shoots, so it is important for him to hunt well. They are very happy with today's catch.

Harald is proud to be a hunter, like his father and grandfathers before him.

A hunter's life

Harald, his wife, their three children and his parents all live together in the house.

Leaving the dogs tied up outside, we go into the Bajares' cabin, and are delighted to find ourselves in a warm and cosy room. There is an oven, two beds, a sofa and a couple of chairs.

Harald built the cabin himself, with money he borrowed from the local council. Each month he pays back some of the loan. The house has two rooms and a kitchen downstairs, and another room upstairs.

As we sit down and drink welcome cups of hot coffee, we ask Harald about his life as a hunter.

"Well," he smiles, "I am 30 now and I have been a hunter since I was 7. I got my first gun for my seventh birthday. Two years later I got my first rifle. I always knew I wanted to be a hunter, even when I was very young. My father was a hunter, and his father before him. Besides, it was the only way to earn any money.

"My father taught me how to hunt. He told me about animals, the ice, sea currents, and the weather. He taught me how to judge the weather, told me of the dangers, and what to do if I got into difficulties," Harald explains.

"The most important thing for a hunter is to get up very early to study the weather, to see what the clouds are like, and in which direction the wind is blowing. In the spring, when you are out in the hunting grounds for several days, you have to be careful of the warm currents under the ice. When the sun is shining, the ice can become very unsafe."

The dogs live outside, chained to the ice. They pull the family's sled.

Hunting is often dangerous, as Harald goes on to tell us.

"I had my first important lesson when I was 14 years old. I had gone hunting seals on my own one morning when I suddenly fell through the ice. I was swimming around for about an hour in the freezing water before I could manage to get up onto the ice again.

"If my father hadn't taught me what

Harald repairs his sled before going on a hunting expedition.

to do, I would have died. I remembered what he'd told me and swam on my back, up onto the ice. I kept trying until I found an ice floe strong enough to carry my weight. Afterward, I ran home to comfort and warmth."

In early spring, polar bears begin to roam on the ice. Harald knows that this is the time of year when the chances of shooting a bear are greatest, so he gets up particularly early.

"I get up at 4:00 a.m. and get home late in the afternoon. I feel disappointed if I don't catch anything. On the other hand, if I come home with a good catch, I feel an inner peace and pride impossible to reach in any other way."

"Three years ago," Harald continues, "I was out with another hunter in two boats. It was September. Suddenly I saw a walrus about 2 kilometers (1 mile) away. My friend shot first, but missed. He shouted 'Shoot!' and I hit it. It took us eight hours to tow the walrus home. It weighed over a ton. There was a party that day. My father knew how to cut a walrus up, and did so with his dagger.

A hunter will stand for hours at a hole in the ice, waiting for a seal to come up to breathe.

We cooked rice with the meat, and all our friends came to share the meal. We kept some for Christmas, and there was still enough left for another four months!"

Harald smiles as he tells this story. He will never forget that day. It helped to make his reputation as a good hunter.

Batseba

Later that evening, when the seal Harald caught has thawed, we go into the kitchen to watch his wife, Batseba, cut up the animal. This is the hunter's wife's traditional role. Using her *ulo* (a special Greenland knife) it takes her just 20 minutes to skin and cut up the seal. The skin will be sold, and the meat will provide the family with food.

When she has finished, we ask Batseba how the family divides the work.

"I take care of whatever animals Harald catches. I also look after the cooking, cleaning and washing," she explains, "but we share the job of looking after the children. When Harald sees I need help, he lends a hand and, of course, his parents do the same. His mother, Emma, helps me a lot. She loves the children, and she's very good with them. I'm glad we all live together. We get on well and help one another whenever we can."

We are curious to know how Batseba and Harald met each other.

Harald smiles, "Well, Batseba was visiting our village when we met each other for the first time. It was at a dance and music evening in the village hall. We liked each other, and lived together for two years. We found out that we couldn't do without one another, so we got married

Batseba expertly skins and cuts up the seal that her husband has caught.

She is also kept busy looking after three sons. This is Åge, her youngest child.

and moved into my parents' house."

"Are you never afraid when your husband's out hunting?" we ask.

Batseba shakes her head. "No. Harald is an expert hunter with a lot of experience. Even though he might sometimes be in danger, I know he can take care of himself. That's why I'm not afraid," she replies.

"I'm a Christian, and I trust in God," adds Harald. "I feel that He has something to do with it on the days when I have a good catch. That time I escaped from the ice-cold water, I felt God's presence more strongly than ever before or since. And I'm not afraid of bears – I'm more afraid of my fellow men."

Harald and Batseba are obviously happy together.

"I am satisfied," Harald says. "The only thing I could wish for is some furniture for the home, and maybe a fishing boat. But the money we get from selling sealskins is not enough for us to buy anything like that, and the prices of things keep rising."

Batseba makes beautiful pieces of Greenlandic beadwork.

Harald and Batseba share the job of looking after the children.

Emma

Jonas and Emma, Harald's parents, used to live in the hut that you can see behind them.

Harald's parents, Emma and Jonas, have been listening intently to all that has been going on, and helping to keep the children amused while we talked. Now we want to ask them all about Kap Dan in "the old days." Have they seen changes in the way of life here?

"Oh yes," smiles Emma. "Things have changed so much. We never had a wooden cabin like this one. Jonas and I used to live in a hut made of peat, just one room lined with wooden planks and sealskin. You can still see the hut outside, behind this house. That is where Harald was born.

"The village was much smaller then. There were only four houses. We got our heating and lighting from oil lamps that we made from hollowed-out stone. Now there are lots of houses, and a store, a church and a school."

Emma had seven children, only three of whom are still alive. She remembers clearly how hard life was in those days.

"I used to get up about 2:00 in the morning and work until 11:00 at night. It had to take care of the catch, look after our children and dogs, sew boots for my man and children, and sew skins for our kayak. No bit of the seals went to waste.

I made sacks from sealskins which I filled with seal blubber and buried in July. In October I dug up the sacks and used the blubber to make oil for heating and lighting. I also made sewing thread from the seals' flippers. In the winter I washed and softened sealskins.

"It was a much harder life then, but it was a good life. There were plenty of animals to hunt. Now there are not so many. But today we have more money in our pockets and need not starve any more.

"I wouldn't want to change anything. I've been healthy all my life, and happy."

Emma has seen many changes in Kap Dan.

Jonas

Jonas (Harald's father) then tells us about his childhood. His father was a hunter, too, and life was often very harsh.

"I was only 7," Jonas remembers. "We were seven brothers and sisters and we had not eaten for more than fourteen days. It was terrible weather, and we couldn't hold out any longer. We were about to die from hunger. My father went out to shoot something so that we could eat. But he didn't come back. Later we found him just a few paces from the hut. He was dead from exhaustion and frostbite. He had died just as he was about to reach home.

"We children were then parceled out among aunts and uncles. My mother died some years later from tuberculosis, so I had to look after myself."

When Jonas was a child, life was very hard for his family.

Jonas clearly remembers his most successful day, when he caught three polar bears.

Jonas continues by telling us about the best day in his life as a hunter.

"I started early, and by the end of the morning I'd shot two seals. I considered going home, but decided to carry on hunting. Then I saw three polar bears at the ice's edge. They were just as quick in catching sight of me and ran toward an iceberg. I released three of my best dogs and they managed to drive the bears away from the iceberg down toward me. The dogs circled 'round the bears on the ice floe, cutting them off from escape. I fired three shots – and killed all three. That was more than 20 years ago, but I remember it as if it was yesterday."

Harald nods and smiles. That was the time he got his first rifle.

23

The Bajares' children

Henning, Kristian and Åge, the Bajares' children, are three years, two years, and one year old, respectively. They are too young to tell us about their feelings. But it is clear that they enjoy having loving parents and grandparents, and are all happy living close together in the cabin. But what sort of life will they lead when they are older?

Harald is in no doubt.

"My sons are not going to be hunters," he says. "It's too hard and nowadays there are not enough animals. My sons are going to have a proper education, so that they can get work. First of all they'll have to study hard at school. I want them to be happy, and that won't be as hunters. My trade is a dying trade. I know I'm the last hunter in the family."

Harald is sad at this thought, for although hunting is a hard life, he loves his work and is proud to belong to such an ancient tradition.

Certainly, Harald and Batseba's sons will have better educational opportunities than their parents had. In a few years, they will all be pupils at the school at Kap Dan.

During Harald's lifetime there have been many changes, as attempts have been made to bring the traditional lifestyle of Greenlanders into line with the standards of Denmark, the country that

Emma enjoys looking after her grandchildren and playing games with them.

Schoolchildren playing on the ice at Kap Dan.

still "owns" Greenland. The Danish government has now set up schools in all of Greenland's towns and villages, mostly with Danish teachers. Medical services, better housing and other modern improvements have been introduced. But this means that the older ways of life are threatened.

Greenlanders are now taking greater control of their own country. No doubt Harald's children will see many more changes in their time.

Henning and Kristian will soon go to school. Harald does not want them to be hunters.

Village life

We asked Harald and Batseba what it is like to live in Kap Dan, surrounded for most of the year by ice and snow. Isn't it lonely, we asked?

"Oh no, village life is very friendly," Batseba explains. "We love visiting each other's houses for a good chat and a cup of coffee!"

There are no daily newspapers in Greenland and no television broadcasting, so communities still make most of their own entertainment. In Kap Dan there is a meeting hall, which is a social center for everyone. The women's club meets there to knit and embroider and chat. Once a week the young people meet there to dance to music provided by a tape recorder.

"Even though my working week is about 80 hours long," explains Harald, "I still have time for my hobbies of skiing and soccer."

On Sundays the Bajares go to the little wooden church at Kap Dan.

"And I go to the women's club to sew and do beadwork," says Batseba, "and I knit clothes for the children."

Religion is very important too. Each Sunday they go to the little wooden church in Kap Dan, where the school-teacher acts as minister and preaches, plays the piano and conducts the hymn singing.

Outside the church is the graveyard, where wooden crosses stand in the snow

There are very few roads in Greenland, so helicopters are frequently used.

and pots of plastic flowers decorate the graves. No real flowers could survive in this climate.

Although there is no doctor or police-man in the village, a "flying" police force and medical service is provided by helicopter from the town of Angmagssalik, along the coast.

A farewell meal

Before we go, Batseba promises to make us the family's favorite dish – Greenland seal. This is made by cutting up fresh seal meat and boiling it in a pot with water and salt. After about an hour, the meat is taken out and served on a large dish.

We all sit down together to eat the seal that Harald caught. Batseba pours out glasses of water for us to drink with our meal. The boiled seal has a surprisingly sweet taste.

Whenever Harald catches a seal, the family has this dinner. Like other Greenlanders their diet consists mainly of seal, fish, dried fish, whale and walrus meat. In the old days, as Jonas has told us, people died of starvation when the hunters came home empty-handed, or the weather was too severe for hunting. Nowadays, however, they can buy food, imported from Denmark, in the local store. Besides food, the store supplies them with clothes, rifles, ammunition and sewing equipment.

After our meal we sit and talk, but it is soon time for us to make our way back to the airport. The family gathers at the door to wave goodbye to us as Harald drives us away by dog sled. We wave back and thank them for their kindness and hospitality.

As we race across the ice, the village of Kap Dan grows fainter and fainter, until it is just a line of brown smudges on a white landscape.

Batseba prepares the meal in the kitchen.

The Bajares sit down together to enjoy a traditional dinner of Greenland seal.

Facts about Greenland

Size: The area of Greenland is about 2,175,600 square kilometers (840,000 square miles). It is the largest island in the world.

Capital City: The capital city is called Nuuk in Greenlandic and Godthåb in Danish.

Population: There are about 52,000 people in Greenland, 90 percent of them living on the west coast.

Language: Both Danish and Greenlandic are spoken. Greenlandic is a dialect of the Inuit (Eskimo) language.

Money: Greenlanders use the same currency as in Denmark, the Danish Kroner.

Religion: Most Greenlanders are Christian and belong to the Greenlandic Church, headed by the Lutheran Archbishop of Copenhagen, in Denmark.

Climate: Temperatures in Greenland vary, but most of the country is inside the Arctic Circle and is very cold. Average temperatures in January in the north are −35°C (−31°F). Average temperatures in the summer in the south are 7°C (45°F). Snow falls throughout the year.

Government: Greenland is a self-governing territory of Denmark. It has a law-making body called the Landsting, with 21 members. It also sends two members to the Danish parliament. Danish authority in Greenland is represented by a High Commissioner.

Education: The education system is based on that of Denmark, but the main language used in schools is Greenlandic. In 1983 there were 100 schools in Greenland with 10,700 pupils and 1,100 teachers.

Agriculture: Some sheep and reindeer can be kept on the coastal areas, and a very few crops are grown.

Industry: Fishing and seal hunting are the most important industries. A little mining is also done for lead, zinc and cryolite.

Glossary

Blubber The thick layer of fat under the skin of some sea animals, such as the seal. It helps the animal to keep warm in the sea, and provides Greenlanders with fat and fuel.

Current Fast-flowing section of a sea or river.

Frostbite Serious, sometimes fatal, damage caused to the body by extremely cold temperatures.

Greenlanders Inhabitants of Greenland; a mixture of peoples descended from the Inuit (Eskimos) of North America and Europeans from Norway and Denmark.

Greenlandic The language of Greenland; a dialect of the Inuit (Eskimo) language.

Inuit The Eskimo people of North America.

Kayak A canoe-like boat made from sealskins.

Peat Rotted plants, dug out of boggy land and used as a building material and a fuel.

Snowcat A vehicle with caterpillar tracks, designed for use on snow and ice.

Snowmobile A vehicle designed for use on snow and ice.

Tuberculosis (TB) A serious, and sometimes fatal, disease affecting the lungs. It was once common but has now been largely wiped out by the use of modern drugs.

Ulo A sharp knife used in Greenland to cut up and skin animals.

Index

Acknowledgments

All the illustrations in this book were supplied by the authors, with the exception of the following: Bryan and Cherry Alexander 6, 15 and 23. The maps on pages 7 and 9 were drawn by Bill Donohoe.